Water

D1253170

OTHER BOOKS BY ROBERT VANDERMOLEN

COLLECTIONS OF POETRY
Blood Ink
The Invisible Lost Book of Deep Ocean Fish
Variations
The Pavilion
Circumstances
Along the River
Of Pines (chapbook)
Night Weather (chapbook)
Peaches
Breath

ANTHOLOGIES
Michigan Signatures
Traveling America with Today's Poets
Tigris & Euphrates
From A to Z
Contemporary Michigan Poetry
A Visit to the Gallery
The Sumac Reader
The Talking of Hands
New Poems from the 3rd Coast
March Hares
Poetry and Painting in the Galleries
History of Lincoln Lake
Growing a Masterpeice
Thin Ice (prose)

Water

Robert VanderMolen

MICHIGAN STATE UNIVERSITY PRESS ▪ *East Lansing*

Copyright © 2009 by Robert VanderMolen

⊖ The paper used in this publication meets the minimum requirements
of ANSI/NISO Z39.48-1992 (R 1997) (Permanence of Paper).

 Michigan State University Press
East Lansing, Michigan 48823-5245

Printed and bound in the United States of America.

15 14 13 12 11 10 09   1 2 3 4 5 6 7 8 9 10

LIBRARY OF CONGRESS CATALOGING-IN-PUBLICATION DATA
VanderMolen, Robert.
Water / Robert VanderMolen.
p. cm.
ISBN 978-0-87013-846-1 (pbk. : alk. paper)
1. City and town life—Middle West—Poetry. 2. Country life—Middle
West—Poetry. 3. Middle West—Poetry. I. Title.
PS3572.A4285W37 2009
811'.54—dc22
                      2008029577

Book and cover design by Sharp Des!gns, Inc., Lansing, Michigan
Cover art courtesy of iStockphoto.com.

green
press
INITIATIVE Michigan State University Press is a member of the Green
Press Initiative and is committed to developing and en-
couraging ecologically responsible publishing practices. For more infor-
mation about the Green Press Initiative and the use of recycled paper in
book publishing, please visit www.greenpressinitiative.org.

Visit Michigan State University Press on the World Wide Web at
www.msupress.msu.edu

for Deb again
and
for my friends

~

CONTENTS

Part 1

Fishing at the Falls

Beer is cold in the water
A breeze is cold behind us,
A draft from shadow, the wall eaten under,
A moody huddling, where rock
Has fallen from the upper lip
Like crumbs (we imagine)
Until rock meets rock
At the rubble of river

How we've turned to fiction,
Says Dick—all this hunger,
Pitchy with wonder, came full
Circle in a way . . .

There's no assuaging his assumptions

Pines hanging by roots
A hundred feet above us

Shuddering volume, illuminated mist,
Dull bugs rising, tranquility
Coupled with an awkward faith—

Leading threads of comparison,
Of expertise, he continues,
When daylight spread her hips
Into a grand generosity . . .

Yeah, I say, but who's going
To pay for it now

~

I refuse to submit, he whispers
Just before he dies. Small
In his wife's arms, like an irregular pillow
With fish inside

Those strenuous tubes drooping.
The odor.
Birches standing
Like broom handles outside his wide window

∿

Spunky cold in the cemetery,
Someone reading Tennyson
Too slowly—bright sand
Tossed over ice and snow.
The lack of substantial trees,
Markers dating from lumber days—
We're knotted on one side
In front of straw rising behind the casket,
In front of winter, in front of sitting
Past midnight, shelves, and ashtrays,
Carpet, the telephone dry,
Wires banging against the siding.
I wanted to say, the knowledge
That we were friends
Always made me feel better. But I didn't.
Rather,
It was you bumping over the hill
Honking in the dark, firing
Your Spanish-American War pistol.
A grocery sack with steak and a bottle
Or two of wine

Dated

1.

The postcard said
Something muffled.
I was more intrigued
By the cover photo
Of three Great Lakes liners

In snow—
You couldn't tell
Where the ice and wharfs combined,

Those enormous steel hulls—

2.

I had a beer

It's an old house,
The smell of old houses in winter

Our woolen leggings

3.

In the spring
I took my wife to a hill above the postcard

Then to the river

There's a hotel room
With a massive mirror across one wall.
A cubed nightstand made of mirrors.
Mirrors covering doors

What do you think of this,
I said on the balcony, above the water—

> The sun pops,
> We change our clothes,
> Everyone admires the scenery

4.

I remember the time
I wrote a highly-charged erotic letter to my girlfriend,
A positive calming one to my mother

Then posted them in the wrong envelopes

5.

It's a secret thing

Ducks squawking.
Insects darting and bowing. Bats at dusk.
These ripples. Why the postcards
Are so popular

6.

Past broken buildings
Down a sandy track growing thinner.
Wind streams out of the west,
Cold and shivers of rain . . .

> I had to back the car
> All the way out finally.
> Loose planks, mortar crumbling.

The hill dropped sharply to the river.
The sand greasier

My wife decided to walk

    7.
The liners have been gone for years.
They would be gone this late in the season anyway.

Just gone, one morning missing

The Fondness

You're drifting, she said
Between reality and the pseudo-event.
It's like a new cotton nightgown,
Printed with songbirds, which one touches . . .
It's as simple as that. Could-a-beens
Don't buy you a beer. The sash and sway
Of platitudes . . . No, he replied, I'm concerned
With fondness . . . She made a deprecating
Gesture, how wisdom has abandoned the school
System, how pleasantness has abandoned
The borders of towns. She said, it's like
Busts and statues in the back corridor
Of the art museum, suspended dust, pigeon shit
Bleeding over the windows, the red light
Of exit . . . You don't really feel that way
Do you? He asked. I've had some misfortunes,
She answered faintly, raised her finger
Raised her voice, disasters in fact.
Before returning to her tea
She brushed both her earrings, as if to see
If they were still attached.
But Jennifer, he pleaded . . . Her flat hand
Stopped him, don't talk to me of fondness,
Don't quote Rilke either

A Snowy Evening

I didn't mean to sit in a bar
With someone I barely knew,
Running my finger through water
Marks like some sage historian
With a brandy problem—an archaeologist
I met once . . . Well, that's beside
The point, his theory died with him,
The waitress who lived with him
Couldn't read. What seems so clear
In retrospect, circling nigh like an osprey,
Over meadows and hedges, the lost soft
Colors of youth . . . Or friends grown
Estranged, particular towns gone touristy.
Odd ramparts rising up sides of a wind-blown bluff—
Not ruins in the traditional sense, you understand,
But the mystery that clears itself up
At the end of the book, I've always loved you, she said.
Gulls fluttering that looked like napkins.
The hill opposite, like a bear's back—
As predictable outcomes deflate, fall into water like bark
When no one but children are watching . . . What is
Scratched, discolored and small . . . so small you have
To crouch close to the painting, an arrowhead perhaps
Among the chickens, flat pebbles, bearded men
Passing one of several painted gates

Sardines and Pears

Down a long plain of skin,
The headlands, a starkness
Without a crease of emotional
Need or sordidness. Cavalry
Clomping down the street outside.
This imbalance.
This lack of salt, this perspective
With which one should have stayed
On the other side of a window, or table.
Copper colored walls, a print of men
Netting sardines.
The languid weather of it.
Perfume that opens a magazine.
Across the dresser and door
Triangles of light . . .

Water

The wrong answer to the wrong question . . .
Opens across that Magritte mystery of lawn
Into trees, when a sawed-off shotgun appeared in the hand
Of a man who once worked in the sheriff's Dept,
A miscalculation,
Women's faces in the window,
Feeling soft earth, water trickling from a shadow—
I hadn't considered this in years

Musky with attention, the young couple across the road,
Carafe of orange liqueur, appear at the door,
Chumming for gossip,
For dreams—
Pink complexion of water,
Ripples from tied boats, a leaf fluttering loose:
Before the dogs wake and clatter down the aged
Wooden steps.
Pretty soon it is noon and you've done nothing

Regarding Calm

Air rising off water—
You absorbed it like the attention
Of an attractive friend. A fragrance,
A kindness, an open-air suggestion.
Digressions abound, as they used to say.
On Lake Michigan Emily switches
To automatic pilot, goes below
To read her O'Brian novel. Sips
What she sips. My dog Katie, a Newfoundland,
No doubt dreams of something she's never seen.
While tree frogs answer tree to tree.
In Savannah that year the ladies
Purchased me a Panama hat, knitted me
A cotton vest. How much better
They thought I appeared—though I was fast
Approaching the status of toy-boy.
Pilfering small thoughts
From magazines and television. Pills from purses.
Bumps of crows lining black railings.
While moonlight oscillated through clouds
Of approaching winter.
Pressure on the ears and tongue,
As intrigue permeates detail
In unlikely ways. Security versus hopelessness.
Ambition in search of irony.
With echoes trailing back to a littered shore,
To fishermen, burly in waders and wool,
Snagging salmon in front of headlights.
To acorns rolling from a dune behind
The piano factory (converted into apartments,
A micro-brewery) where Emily keeps
Her clothes and correspondence,

Whatever secrets she owns. The squeaking
Of schooling bats over the Methodist Church
That turn into shrapnel spiraling up.
To a cack-handed comment, to a lazy breeze
Stirring the harbor. To a cemetery in pines,
To pace-makers ticking under sod.
A fox posing at the iron gate . . . as the weeks
Loitered with no ill effects.
But hardly anyone agrees any longer, I said.
They don't have to, she replied,
What it comes to, after the squall of doubt,
Is how we feel afterwards . . .

Craters

1.

One gazes at the inland lake
After speed boats have quit. A solitary heron
Stiffening into reeds. When light
Humps around the tamarack
On the far shore
Water fossilizes
Briefly

Rick said
There are puddle lakes with craters in them,
If you study a map
They run in a line across the county
Connecting like dots—I'm not saying
This is one—but my grandfather told me
At the turn of the century
Someone dumped stumps in a crater,
They popped up floating in several other lakes.
These were big white pine stumps . . .

Such went the beer talk
Among the retired teachers.
How the church was vandalized,
All they knew was what was smeared on the pews.
A man and a woman in a rowboat
On a hazy day, drifting out where the island used to be,
Who would have guessed he would have snapped like that.
Fireflies pricking lilacs,
A faint disturbance of water—

There aren't any craters in this lake
Said Larry

I've fished every inch.
He shifted in his wooden chair
So solidly
It lurched north across the planking.
I'm with you, said Ron, gripping the railing.
Bats darting out
From the fireplace chimney above them.
Inside
The women were stirring their own

2.

When confronted with acute anticipation
He said to his friend, it's better
To screw your mouth shut, cloak ambition:
Keep your powder dry

The same day as the stump queen
Was crowned at the festival, the finals
Of the tractor pull—at the other corner
Of the lake, into shadows of cedar
Dragonflies rising and falling, vapors gathering
Among a row of half-hidden cottages

She said, sometimes we miss
Les Paul and Mary Ford, they had such nice names—
Splash of a bass, a neighbor shutting down his
Lawnmower, how one gravitates
To the other side of sound

The Beast

Beside the stanchions
Elevating his moldy boat
Old Tobin was gaunt
Slouching in his captain's chair
In weeds, the shed door ajar
Permanently, exposing
That treasure of tossed
Vodka bottles
Glinting in a shaft
Of sun through aspen.
In the 1880s
He continued, it was captured
Hauled away to Greenville
Caged outside the jail . . .
When it was sick of crowds,
It muscled its way one night
Bending bars like soft plastic . . .
I lost the progression
Of his tale in the heat,
Watching the dangling
Growth on the tip of his tongue,
Something out of a Hawthorne
Story, a slight worm
As in a mouth of an angler fish.
Rotten breath
Creeping out of the swamp,
He was saying, gesturing vaguely
Across water, where birch
Keep toppling . . .
Rotting breath of darkness, yes, yes.
It's grown more elusive since . . .
He reached for his cup

On the upturned cinder block.
I see, I said, but where did
The farmer's ferry, the forgotten ferry,
Cross exactly—the query
Which had brought me to visit—
Young man, he growled,
Have you never learned
To listen

Willow

Or smoke billowing
On a cross-cut past the deck

Towards Doris'—a sick shameful smell

Though at a distance, how can I put this?

Watching Richard feed his aggressive
Fire, dancing back like a bullfighter

The water behind him a liverish color,
Another storm piling in—

Kent following me up the stairs
Uninvited, baits and lures, flashlight fishing . . .

A funny little twinkling in the flowers

Clump of black-eyed susans

In this muggy August hour
My appetite beginning . . .

Kent, leaning on the outer railing,
Referring to his ex-wife,
Her boyfriend, as the dog and pony show

His doughy face of doubt

A Town

Ten degrees below zero this morning, he writes to his friend—
Like everyone else who writes to friends in these parts,
Trees, brush and snow, only something like a cardinal
Shows any spunk, as in a Xmas card opened in Florida
Or San Diego—the dirty green tufts at peaks of white pine
Complete it. Sipping soup or poking through a catalog
Imagination is at its low water mark, though it shouldn't be.
It shouldn't be so brittle, like aging shelf ice, like bones
In the back room, deer bones no doubt, ribs and tibias—
With thoughts like stale crackers, cold cracked boots.
Mucus dried. Men recalling deer camps of their youth.
Women hunched over with paper packages on the street
Below the hill blotched by sliding sand, and dark disks
Of earth and roots where maples have toppled. An entire world
Of contrivances caught in slush, falling in blocks over
The short falls where the power company once had a generator
Which detached one night in an explosion of block and cable,
Sparks like stars, about the time trains stopped running north,
Though that was several baseball seasons ago—when the governor
Still came home in summer with his lonely daughter,
To the yard where a statue stood peeing water behind
A brick wall—a square napkin, a round fat candle
At the end of the wing of the tavern where the doctor,
The mayor and the constable meet for steaks and margaritas,
Sound of the river sliding by and over the revetments—
Though there is still concern for Margaret so long missing
From her journey to Cincinnati, Ed's Margaret that is.
Didn't he find some Hopewell jewelry in those mounds
On his property? I don't believe it amounted to much, said Jake.
But he's an odd duck. I remember standing in their kitchen,
It was so dark you could barely see him grinding sausage, the old grinder
Bolted to the table. What did he do with it, the copper jewelry,

I mean? Sold it downstate, said Jake. But even the minister
Won't talk to him since he shot the poacher. Reinder opened
His hands, as if bread was ready to float down from the ceiling.
A tin ceiling needing some repair and cleaning. Not that the parson
Has much to crow about since that episode with Mrs. Dish.
Well, yes, but there is a difference I think. Being in the war and losing
His eye, said Tom. It was our luck that brought us our worry,
He once said. All three considered fate for a moment. Jake lit
A cigar. I grew up near Margaret you know. She told me long ago
That in the middle of the night she found her way to the outhouse
Pulled up her nightshirt and sat on a chicken. Ha ha, laughed Reinder,
That could explain quite a bit . . .

Bug Bites

He's a bit rough around the edges,
It read . . .

The pink of the lake's surface at 9 P.M.
Like color on a picture postcard
60 years earlier—an emotion hidden
Briefly from view
(behind palmettos) . . .

The latter part of the message (of course)
Crudely crossed out . . .

Above branches of a Chinese Elm
The V of geese alter into a W
Heading north where silence is more certain

Men make such projects
With mystery and conspiracy,
When in general there isn't much there,
Said Mrs. Dixon

Part 2

Three Stories

1. BLUEBIRDS & APPLES

Of bluebirds and orioles
Singing for Uncle Kelly

Born guilty (in everyone's movie)

Who stops under a sycamore
For a sip of Old Grand-Dad

Buxom Miss Daisy
Teaching Sunday school

Two rows of daunted boys
She swivels

Pauses at the window

The shuttered library
Across monument park

At fall leaves, everything in movement
Cement and bronze

A trickle of sweat
Meeting elastic—

A little nap in the restroom
Thinks the teenage football player

Bruised from the game the night before
More bruised

By a scuffle in the parking lot
(after the dance), the tentative

First sensations of gonorrhea
What will he tell his girlfriend

His mother, he'd rather
Shoot himself hunting

He'd rather sleep—

His girlfriend Susan
Staring at her breasts

In the bath, a holy steam
Rising from water

To the mirror, to the roof
To the head of the valley

Past billboards, nut trees,
A swale

Where the sun is less oily—

Ruts of a trail

Where one reflects on the nature
Of fate (before fate lost its

appetite),
Before Uncle Kelly returned from China

And Miriam begot Miss Daisy

2. IN THE '90S

Linked to the pomp
Of morning

Tourists,
Bright hankies of sound

Dipping, gliding,
Carrying over striations

Of bay. Just us
Leaving on the ferry.

At the reception
I recall the psych prof

Saying, the rats
Are never wrong

Runnels of thunder
Muffled light

From a range of hills.
Small movements of mice

Put me to sleep again.
Sand stains

And cloves of erotica
Before the vaulting

Doldrums.
New silt and old leaves

Before things turned serious
At the tail of the decade . . .

Authorities
From downstate

Pushing back their chairs
From the table, sighing . . .

Or when the Chevy truck
Ahead of me

Spun like a bottle
Kicked by a drunk.

In that narrow room
With their white wine

And white sofa.
Downstairs, a corsage

Of mail stuck in the box . . .

Saliva of ice
Under my feet.

Where was Martha?
When I decided

To sketch her
And paint again

3. THE 8 STEPS

The last beer,
The last plane
Rising milk-white
Without me

⁓

Something too
Regarding the screen door

Hummingbirds working
The meadow

⁓

Moments leap-frogging
Each other
Like ideas
Until the last
Worst one

⁓

The aunts dead
And Mondrian
Old-fashioned

Whereas once
There were garter snakes
In the rhododendron

~

Alleys of sour,
A tapping of hard
Metal
Hanging in the boatyard

On either side
Water sniffs
And retreats
Snail shells, pebbles
Like beads

~

Meanwhile
Listening to Django Reinhardt
On the stereo

No berms of doubt
Up north or not
This lasted several years

~

D. H. said, think of air
As invisible dirt

It's like piling sunk
Into soft uncertain ground,
Said A. K., speaking
Of something else

~

On brown-grey steps
A large toad, nearly the same color
Taking its time, moving up

The purples and blues of habit
Where Doris had been leaning

Commerce

Rust in the pipes, in the food,
In the air of the storeroom,
Virginia creeper covering the screens

Where the men peer, disease in the air,
Just what the ladies fear,
They can't win and they fuckin' know it,
Says Frank.
Or as they stand and smile for the tv woman
Next to the camera. All these years
And we're still heroes

⁓

The rest of life always less noisy.
Cleats
On concrete where the ball field
Turns into factory property.
All of it, behind the heat,
Behind the sawdust of breath,
Behind the torpor

⁓

Stepping to the curb
From the bistro, youthful windows
Higher up where music pounds.
The ladies know all about it—

Angry rain on a copper roof

A pattern of nails
Imbedded
In a beech's trunk—

Near fields
Where condos are rising,
Empty hayracks in moonlight

The women applaud,
But the men have grown agitated,
Fingering their car keys. Losing their gravity—

Slippery road of sweat,
Puzzling your way to forgetfulness

⁓

Cul-de-sac of stiff air, country good-will—
With everything they thought they'd left
Dangling in an alley, colloquies of sunlight
On scarred block

Everything resolved.
Bricks set so carefully
Into moist ground . . .

⁓

A recurrence

A sort of ticker-tape,
Bid and asked
Popping like a stick down a picket fence

Time

John Wayne cocking his hip
In Marlene Dietrich's dressing room.
You're a big palooka, she says
Eyeing him up and down, lighting
A smoke. Ma'am, he replies,
Then hesitates, growing leery . . .
She hikes her dress to reveal
A watch strapped to an upper thigh.
We have time, she announces

~

A spiral on the tree trunk
Resembles an Asian woman
Dancing—and why not?
I'd sat on the same stump
For three and a half hours

Dead trout on the beach
Salted with sand

Or staring at the dark hair on her arm
In the barn, the mounting
Nervousness of the horses

~

You get to a point
Where you slide sideways
Like a truck on wet clay—

Afterwards, tilted in
This natural ditch
In woods, it's like you

Knew it was going to happen
Only you wouldn't admit it

Some of these situations
End up much worse than others,
He said

~

Flipping through an argument
Days later, that subtle pressure
For equilibrium

Water filling the claw-foot tub
Outside. At noon
Leaning in the cabin doorway,
Grosbeaks wander the ground
For what's alive and coming
To the surface

Whispering

The susurration at night grows malicious
As it should—the marsh is now marinas—
In that mixed light, gulls standing on pilings,
Soft maples where the streets end,
Ducks gliding, fish nipping the surface.
The water moils. Everyone was once
Young and lonely as well, when hairstyles
Were different. Too many miles on him,
The woman remarks, in the soda fountain
Off the short deck above water, insects
Spinning the hanging bulbs. He's not
That old, says her companion. My point exactly,
She replies

After Lunch

You even begin to sound like someone else,
He complained, a realtor with a nervous
Tick for instance, someone who hasn't sold
A property in 15 months. On the one hand,
After 17 years of accumulation,
Said his friend, you end up like a Xmas grapefruit
In March—I've lived there—sulking for sun,
Rain or something. Yet with the other
You coddle impatience, a tick under your shirt sleeve . . .
That raspberry of pain you can't discuss.
The calm before an explanation—
Time ticks for no one.
Do you remember when people used to talk like that?
Grandfather slouched under an awning
Lighting a cigar, or studying
The length of his tie. He looked
Like one of those detectives in Dallas
When Kennedy was shot

The Interview

A mazed sky.
When I meant to concentrate on all
The splendors and depths of modern commerce . . .
What do you say, she asked, clicking her pen.
That net, I answered precisely, has a lot
Of holes in it. All nets do, she said,
Touching her lipstick at the high point
Of her lower lip
(I was married to someone like that once,
which offered some comfort . . .)

~

Sharp edge of sensation, sorely felt,
Dulled in time by ambition, sap screeching
To a halt. She was staring, I realized,
At my hands creating a small tent.
Dear, she replied, the wastes of time
Forsake no one—there's no defense . . .
Sounds like an exciting proposition, I returned.
Up north tamarack were dropping needles.
A porcupine was wrinkling its mouth
To gnaw a new grip for my maul . . .

Joke

There was that joke of so-and-so's mother
And aunt driving all that way to visit him
Only he'd left shortly before on the bus
To the city, to home, a shameful misunderstanding.
Well, what were they to do. His roommate
Offered them a drink and a bowl of potato chips . . .
It's a great story when you're young. The son
So innocent, his roommate less so.
Though I'll admit it still bothers me
Sometimes at night when the air cleaner
Hisses with dirt, the chipping sound of the fire.
Back when we were poor no one trusted
Anyone—when they did, they shouldn't have.
I see that now. Rooms opening into other rooms.
The weather more dramatic. Outside the glass
Old mountains holding old granite . . .
Just a slow settling over time.
Burning cigarettes, slack skin,
Bargain shoes, bargain purses . . .
I've heard enough, she said,
Were you the roommate or the son?

Of the River

Sound of water
Rushing under ice
At the bulge of river
Tugboats frozen at the quayside,
The MaryAnn, the largest,
Closest to where I stand
Under a toy-colored sky.
Nothing in motion
Or wanting to be, I felt
Like one of the professors
Of my youth, whiskey-breathed
And coy, patter of jargon,
Verse that didn't suck
Creamed herring from a salad fork.
Her bottom is more noticeable
Than her top, said Dean French,
Regarding my love at the time.
But I recovered. Photos
Rarely do justice to the real thing.
Don, captain of the MaryAnn,
His head buoyed above his collar
Like a turtle's, Yesiree he announces,
It's good to keep your dobber up.
I agreed, moving as far
From him as I could
Watching the street and sudden
Pelts of snow, out of nowhere
Into what had been shadow
Between shops and warehouse yards.
Even the dune hidden.
A throaty laugh of wind.
Imagining her in bed with someone else,
Looking the same as you see her

Getting Purchase on Ice

That was a terrible time
When I returned from Canada

Found you in bed with the landlord.
Ha, she breathes

Black hair with flashes of white,
Expectations wound with a piety

⁓

Elizabeth says, I've simplified,
Made order for myself

It's amazing what's happened

I don't even think about it.
(lying, of course)

What about Iris?

She asks.

       Past willows, swans in open water—

Elizabeth
Moving in and out of enemy territory
Like a courier

⁓

You weren't any better, she says.

With dark bark of winter trees,
Hanging pine—a swivet
Out of nothingness. Shadow—

25 years,
I'm still hitching my breath

～

We took a walk on the country road
From the lake to the violin maker's house
For schnapps.
Sun out again, quiet, gravel slightly frozen,
A lip of dry snow

Toucans

Meanwhile in Costa Rica the volcano smokes
Toucans glide down to the banana plantation—
For the moment everything is relaxed.
It is snowing in Michigan, but I'm thinking
Of the newspaper story in September,
Two parrots building a nest on a silo
In Montcalm County—Guido points out
Alulu shadings above the coverts,
Assuming I'm a birder.
I like their beaks. Though am somewhat more
Interested in the volcano. Guido asks
For another malt liquor. He needs, he says
To return to San Francisco for surgery—
Turns out we know the same neighborhood
And pubs. He talks of California girls.
This swirl of old habits and parks,
As in the feathering of dreams
Where everything's altered but names—
The toucans are sometimes poisoned here

Guido touches the scar on his neck
Deb is kneeling, examining a beetle
The size of her fist. The birds darken
The horizon at dusk. In North Beach once,
Everything shifting beneath my boots,
I stepped from the curb at dusk into a turmoil of gulls

A City

A city buried under mud—
Earthquake followed by water
Surging up a narrowing passage

An ancient chronicle remarked
How one could peer at domes and spires
Under a bright and spacious lagoon

The question is, she asked herself,
Whether the sea had risen or the landscape sunk

Ordinarily, she was too embarrassed
To say what she meant. Taking a shower
With leaves nearly covering the window,
A congress of birds on the hillside . . .

As fast as you wane your child grows,
Grandmother said,
Salting her beer

Oregon

Such a nice stomach,
Smooth, almost hairless,
But when I look up
Your face is stretched
Like a circus clown's,
Is it embarrassment or
Some untoward tension.

In late afternoon
This switchback
With stones arranged and colored
Like rattlesnakes—how lonesome the adventurer—
Such heat on the slope.
Yet the cobalt blue of the river, down there,
Peeking through fir.
How startling the view

Sun on water

Part 3

Warm Day in March

Who could have guessed
That those would be the days
We talk about, the woman said.
I was eight inches from her window,
Noticing her hands were paper-like
(her friend's I couldn't determine).
A soft tune was playing.
The light changed and they accelerated
In their Jaguar south down Division—
Followed by a short convoy
Of municipal trucks, diesel fumes
Seeking every orifice—
Until I continued strolling east.
The abandoned art deco building
Where I think the Chamber of Commerce
Once huddled under cigarette smoke
Or was it the Association of Furniture
Manufacturers . . .
Heading to meet Hank and Larry.
Sun blinking on brick and asphalt
Behind the used and rare bookstore
Where wrappers scuttle back and forth
Below an aging Communist symbol
Spray-painted on a parking lot post
In the 1970s, reddish on off-white,
What youngish students at the community
College might suspect, without much thought,
Is a cattle brand, or logo for vodka,
Maybe a warning for unprotected sex.
Clouds rapidly expanding overhead
So that the top of the building acquires
An induced movement . . .

Though I couldn't seem to get rid
Of the regret I woke to, a splint of light
On the suet feeder, faint stir in the trees,
That it had been a mistake
To have argued with my father all those years
Over religion and politics—
Issues change but fundamentals remain the same—
Not like he'd witnessed the fall of Rome.
Not something I cared to dwell on either
Passing my childhood doctor's office
And crossing the lane to the Cottage Bar

Under the Sky

How it was, after the babies,
One week's vacation at the shore
During late July, trying to isolate
A hummock of time in which to be dazed,
Beer in the mug, the slant of sunsets,
Fried chicken seasoned with sand.
All of us thinner, sweat-dried, more prone
To anger. With a housecat prowling
Through dune grass . . .

And they made a film of it. I've forgotten
The name of the one who played me.
Someone with more hair on his body.
My wife was shorter with a robust bosom.
While a character died reluctantly
Snatched by a rip in the current
And roiled beyond the sandbar
(where brown trout lurked like torpedoes),
Bubbles becoming foam.
We used to joke about monstrous sturgeon
Fish that would slip into shallows
To suck up infants . . .

Eventually we scattered:
Through divorces, disreputable habits,
Windfalls and death.
The actors disappeared too—
Unlike us, they played in the last Westerns,
Never left Montana
After they were cashiered.
Plains rising into a wall of mountains.
I've often considered driving west
After steaming across on the ferry . . .

At the Airport

Chanel stops at size 12, I'll be jiggered
If I'm going to grow larger than that,
Carla confides to an acquaintance.
A roguish merchant peers over his donut.
At the check-through Vickey drops
A plastic bag of jewelry into a refuse bin—
This would later prove puzzling. A dark
Foreign student sits studying his fingernails—
Though he was found to be an evangelical
Christian. The air is still clean and slightly
Chilly. So it's a muzzy mystery
What that scent is blundering through
The rows of plastic seats. Someone claps
As soldiers leave the tunnel descending
To the lobby, but most glance towards
The slits which are windows. Ralph has
His new book in his lap, the back cover
His photo atop a mare: this may help him
Through customs. How else to reach
The islands when you have to, says Martha
Nervously, 20 years of fear stuffed into her
Carry-on. Her daughter nods sagely,
Fingers entwined. Outside, a worker
Is smoking out of view. Hoses snake
To the jet. Baggage tumbles out.
The sky is white with anticipation—
A kind of paleness everyone approves of.
Still, there isn't much talking among
Strangers these days. A flight attendant,
Fiddling with her pen, wishes she'd had
A better night's sleep. The captain coughs into
His very white hand. When I joked

About her lesbian dream, she became
Less forthcoming, he says.
The co-pilot longs for a beer or two.
Otherwise, prospects seem usual . . .

The Confession

Citronella candles burning in vat-like pots.
He always wondered if she recalled
The distance of the evening, wafting odor of powerboats,
Seaweed, a floating perch, something that
Couldn't be identified—she never talked of it again.
He never inquired. For years strolling down to the shore
Through fish flies, sometimes feverish . . .
Swans cruising. Most people aren't special, she explained.
Even flatness has angles, he said. Where did you read that?
It was a mystery he never detected in her eyes.
Most people don't care, she added; I've always felt sorry
For those that do. Which means what exactly, he asked.
Don't be a chump, pour me a cognac.
One begins to doubt detail, moths congregating
On corrugated bark, even sobs of confession—
With sweat, aging water, smothering vegetation,
A flashlight cutting across a brook in cedar,
Something that vaults into rumor
Even when you know better

The Visit

A man with her
That wasn't me,
Said someone who
Looked familiar.
Where, I wondered,
Though I wish
I hadn't asked

~

Not that confession
Ever did me much good.

Waking,
How pleasurable
To be an adult

A bit of color
In the window,
Trees, sound of
A milk man.
Her skin up against me

Muscle

Obsessions, I'd rather read about them—

I had anticipated hiring a detective
But realized I was better off without so many possessions—
Though I may miss the pieces of glass I found
In the ocean, and, of course, those Japanese fishing floats—
Yet I remain curious who he's seeing, that fat bitch
With a nose job, that college slut with long rubbery nipples,
Or do I stay inside, pull the duvet to my chin
In that timeless fashion, coax a little sympathy
Out of the cat—to go through such anguish
When it seems so obvious now, like a math problem,
After being stymied for weeks, watching the sun come
And go, squirrels digging holes—going from A to B
After clearing out the brush, trying to find something
To tie the narrative flow, an aside that masquerades
As passion, the growth in a private garden—

Or was it, as you suggest, a more materialistic fetish,
Something to do with ownership? I can't quite fathom
How others do it. You, as an example. How people say
It's so pleasing to hear an original voice. But nothing
Stays original very long. That Oldsmobile on blocks
The color of our stained river. I don't want original,
I don't want puddingstone, I want marble. I want clarity.
I don't want dead carp, I want speckled trout leaping
Over the rapids like flying fish—

Now that I consider it, I want more than a pound of flesh,
I want his goddamn head on a skewer . . .

Dan and Marcia

In the background a football game on tv,
Birds whisking away across the deck
From the shadow of a local hawk.
But primarily I couldn't stop reflecting
On my wife saying, half-mashed on gin,
She'd like to seduce a woman we know—
Merely to see what would happen—quite a lot,
She suspects, like a cork out of a bottle—
He related, not sodden with apprehension
Or elevated with desire to manage
Such an assignation, but detached
Like a diplomat on vacation in Mackinaw
City. A woman who was almost
His girlfriend years ago, a colleague,
Who I think he still wonders about in the bath.
Someone, I suppose, his wife has noted
Unconsciously as a rival, though I may
Be reading too much into this—they've
Been together a long time. Unless
She has been an accomplice in sordid
Motels or on truck seats—which I doubt,
Though my imagination has shed
All discipline . . . I can see that Tom, said Larry,
Though I'd be inclined to leave this aside.
It's like a bear tapping on the door, you don't
Really want to open it, do you? Not to mention
All the white-knuckled regrets that can't be
Anticipated . . . Are you trying to tell me
This doesn't interest you? Not at all, said Larry,
I'm only indicating that this may be more
Complicated than it appears . . . Rain puddling
Over ice. A curious whine in the wires . . .

Of Neighbors

Spots of brightness through branches. A pulse
Of water running through shallows . . .

Then there are the peonies
In bloom in early June
Before mosquitoes, moving masses
Of gnats. You look back
At the landing, oars over
A shoulder, with an habitual twinge
You can't put a name to,
Something, no doubt, eddying out from childhood—
Even the poppies flying scarlet
Away from Duane's black curlicue fence . . .

How Pierson used to give us
The water temperature at 8 to 10 feet—
Always so much advice.
We often wondered how his wife
Tolerated his presence on the weekends—
A woman who appeared so wise and attractive

And if I don't wake up in the morning
If I never have another morning
It merely means I never have to dress
For work again. Where's the downside?
That was also Pierson . . .

A pod of wood ducks beyond the point
Past water lilies . . .

Painting Shutters

A woman unloading
Her station-wagon

Bobbed hair, a white blouse
I'm not certain

I saw her face
Even her hands

But her skirt
Was tight and black

She moved
Like someone I knew once.

Waiting everyday

Fixing martinis,
Sweeping the floor

Sitting in front of the door
Where palms skipped about

On the boulevard. Such traffic,
All those voices in Spanish

Stanley Ketchel

Maureen descends the gravel path to her mother-in-law's cottage
Holding a bath towel to her hip
In the filtered light of mid-morning.
A clipping of stones, of dragonflies darting
Above weeds to the color of water,
A wooden rowboat with two men fishing,
And through the shade of old-growth oak . . .
East of the gate is a shed

      ~

Smoke from a stove
Sagging into a haze of wonder, the stirring that ushers in
The baggage of Luminist painters
In early September

His brother said, while I was jazzing her
She fell asleep.
That must have been disconcerting, said Stanley,
Though his words were rougher

      ~

Don't make a mystery where there isn't any, he suggested,
Sipping wine he had shipped from Detroit

After rain the lake a milky sheen stretching out to the island.
The store nestled at the edge of water
They called the pavilion

With a broad rut angling towards the bluff
To a shed, his training cabin—just a madman's room
With one madman's window

At Union High School
Where one gazed at the dome of the cathedral. Or slipped out
To perch on rocks by the river across from the flour mills . . .
At Little Pine Island Lake
Jogging through spider webs and mist

Bones in the Trout Pond

The pump chuckles all afternoon
Pulling water from the channel
To the trout pond behind the house

He disappeared wearing his snow-mobile suit
Riding out at night
On the Newaygo prairie

And of course the church broke up
Over the Vietnam business

The sheriff standing in a cane patch
Of marijuana, grinning like a cuckold
Which he was

While the woman never comes out,
She's a blondie, peering
Over the sink through her window

Her boys, and backdrop of orchard

A dry wind mowing through the apples

Local History

In the liquor store one is enchanted by a print
Of bears holding each other's arms, heads slung up
Singing, dancing about a hooded fire—Tony
Behind the counter, has never danced . . .
Just as Michelangelo tussled with the shape
Of a Venus, his impulse was to attach
Breasts to men—
But Gene no longer has an interest in any kind of art.
My wife won't allow him in the house
Since he tumbled down the stairs—Gene who spent
The last war sitting on the bridge in Sault Ste. Marie
Guarding the locks, numb fingers on an icy machinegun . . .
Married a woman
Who became an eminent actress after she left him—
Gene says, how hairy she was in reality. What he
Described of their intimate life
I once found fascinating—
A dead branch like a claw.
Nothing so studied as something honored.
As we pivot in the park around the Civil War monument—
This isn't Florence by any means—
My wife squares her lips,
How wondrous it is to be discreet, the satisfactions
In maintaining a confidence . . .
Sparrows flitting into glass,
Clutter of bodies on wet pea gravel—
Those days when so much rain made the ground squeak
By itself

Cottage in the Country

With tristful care
Stepping here, stepping there
How all the good measures
Leave the months as blank as detours—
As bored as I was, spying
From my room across the pasture
To hers with binoculars.
Her husband so aero-dynamic
As we used to say. And she so sensitive?
I'd been hoping instead
For something like the rococo nude
Or the woman standing at her basin.
Short of work and short of ideas,
Omissible. Though I may have been
Projecting, as my sister implied.
When what one sets out to do gets replaced,
Devolved amongst cicadas, stray peeps
Of hummingbirds. Sand, dust and my boot prints—
At night a porous rain that regrooms
The country lane. The horse-owners
Nodding into cell phones. An idling plane.
She pulls at her bra straps. Dried sweat
And other imperfections. Disgusting, she tells
Herself. I turn away too. Though my notes
Indicate otherwise

Outside Indianapolis

The waitress seems quite pleased to see you,
Bundles over the morning paper—in which
You discover an acquaintance has done well
In scientific circles recently; not to mention
A second or third wife with an ennobling
Inheritance . . . What's amazing is how lucky
Our heroes are in movies, she interrupts,
Mistaking your profile, it seems, for that
Of some paladin—for an instant however
Rolling grasslands with knots of trees
Near boulders, you doff your hat to pioneers
On foot to the fallen buffalo, the sky
A muted yellow. I'm not famous, you say.
I think I've seen you in films, she returns,
Or on tv. Something from a few years ago
Anyway. You're mistaken, I'm afraid,
I'm not slumming. Behind the swinging door
Someone drops a plate. I doubt it, she replies,
Swiveling in her reckless uniform, coffee pot
In hand. That drone of sports and grain futures . . .
Reminding you then of someone known
Back home as Miss Chevy,
Who had been on the school board briefly . . .

Substation

The electrical substation
Is tucked into June,
Hunching behind the suburban tavern,
The Bright Spot,
Where sandlot baseball players
Drink before they go home to wives and insurance

Among a haphazard arrangement
Of red pine and spruce
A gravel drive that dips—you can fathom
A swamp or swale—
Into a crisp morning someone clanking milk pails . . .

Beyond the roof of the bar
The substation seems to be a miniature dormitory,
Half hidden, half dreamy despite itself. Tree frogs and wild grape,
Sedge, the wandering child . . .

Any story you want to plug, just kitty-corner from the supermarket
And C F gas station. A little refuge perhaps,
Another 40 acres untended, owned and neglected by the Power Co.
A night weather station for those who get lost
Or have lost their edge. The station generally padlocked—
Up close, a sort of guard house, humming

Time and Place

Researchers from the university
Sit at coffee in the shop where newspapers
Have spilled onto the wet and sloping linoleum.
A waitress noodling through her apron
Pocket. A dump truck beeping as it
Backs into a mill across the alley.
Humidity seeping into the pores of morning
Where a yellow dog trots, then peeks
Through bluish glass of the door.
The topic being gorgets of slate
And whether they had been for decoration

Just as there had been speculation
As to where the portage had been
Between the Shiawassee and Maple
In order to reach the Grand.
The water table may have been higher
Before the 19th Century, for example.
There was avid interest when talk
Emerged of carving a canal—
Even the old colonels spoke up.
A stentorious wind across autumn
Avenues of mud. Trade, immigration,
And national security. Before fog
Settled over bankers for a season or two
During a panic—
Finally enlightened by railroads...

A clanging of the times. But removed
From town, the quiet of leather.
A maid leaning against a tree in evening
During Indian Summer in a white

Stiff dress. The moon later
Reproduced on magazine covers
And sheet music. Great migrations
Of shadows. The baying of neglect
When one wandered out over the verge
Into swampland and hillocks of tamarack.
While collections were privately gathered
Of plowed up lithic tools, weapons

A Day at the Races

When you wake up after twelve hours
The stove is cold, there's ice in the water bucket
—clouds outside and snow, the noise of a crow,
The only sound; until your wife cries
From an upper bunk, Honey, I'd like some coffee.
Luther chuckles. I nod, excuse myself for the men's room

Next to me stretches a teacher
Who once warned me not to get married
Too early. Elderly now, but having done well
In real estate as a second career. He says
Well, well, as if he can't recall my name.
But buys me a drink and talks of his wayward
Daughter. When he mentions her married last name
I tell him I have met her, but leave off at that . . .
He squints like a badger. In my wife's family, he resumes,
After a jostling by a drunken salesman, there's a
Sort of stupid gene that runs through the whole outfit,
Being half Finnish, half Dutch—or maybe something
Cancelled something . . . I notice a protuberance, a small growth
At the edge of his eye, hanging like a broken thread

I always thought, I say, your daughter had a charming
Personality. He hunches his shoulders. Waking to dread,
The debts of dread—but I couldn't help him.
Neither did I want to. On the way out
I spot my first wife chatting with a small-time gangster—
She flutters a wave my way, a Victorian flutter

Her Friends

Her friends appreciated the vision of her cabin
With covered porch, only the sound of rabbits
Chewing, deer browsing in the dell—
None of them considered acquiring such a retreat
(or anything similar) for themselves however.
Peculiar how it comforted them though,
In their city clothes, meeting for dinner, touching
Hands, the tinkling of glass, of ideas, scattered
Warm smells. Expressing wise affection for her—
Didn't she look well—leaning in to listen.
Perhaps they thought she had lovers strewn
Among the rural poor, off other unnamed paths.
As Beth sat with her camera, blinking with sweat,
Waiting for the light to peak in seriate trees,
She wondered if they actually cared about
Anything they said they cared for. Above
A pond now clogged with cattails. Desultory
Ducks. I mean, if they weren't friends . . .
But this would get her nowhere. Her husband
Wasn't enchanted by the country either. Bob
Didn't like bugs. Untamed weeds. An outhouse.
There was a story she read once of a man
Unsuspicious of his wife—who lived a second
Life—until she died, hit by a cab, in the street
Wearing jewelry and clothes he'd never seen
Her wear. But this could be turned around too,
It occurred to Beth. It could be her discovering
Him at an intersection on South Division.
Could this be true? She ate a semi-warm
Sandwich from a canvas bag, suspecting she was
Foolish to be so distracted. Give her the white
Chirp of morning, a riant dawn, or later

Before an excited fire, a landscape edging in,
Lacking commotion or any reflection . . . shape
Of a sagging barn, branches of scrub elm.
Her bibbed jeans. Her wonderful torpor.
Needing nothing else, save a lazy dog—
Bless him, her friends said, he bought her
A chainsaw for her birthday

Restorations

Inside, they were polishing the floor:
Planks pried from a sunken schooner
Dried out, worm holes intact—so that
If you spilled your drink, some of it
Could possibly drip into the cellar
(which was older than the schooner,
walls of river limestone mixed with brick
of a trading post called Whiskey Centre—
during the War of 1812 partisans
had hidden behind barrels of liquor and flour
though the more successful ones
had tripped at daybreak into the marsh
to suck through reeds—a sort of gunboat
diplomacy gone awry—the Indians kept
changing sides, plus they knew all the forest paths
of escape—their misfortune was in thinking
this was a passing occurrence
like a holiday that only happened once.
the cellar flooded with gore and storm water
as the whole estuary made islands of neighboring
knolls, though by then the Brits had sailed on
to Traverse Bay—or so I've read).
In April the tourists haven't arrived,
We stand on the wharf watching a current
Tug at block foundations of the burnt bridge—
Which can be seen entire on postcards.
As well as party boats of the 1920s,
Artists with easels in the 1930s.
With the return of cruise liners
There is even talk of resuscitating the town band

Turning 50

There was the dog show on tv. Around the corner
Wind was wrestling wires, cedar in the back
Swaying like bulky assassins. Who can
You believe in? Where once there was a barn
Yards now separate like pieces of pie.
Mickey says, despite all these corncobs
Of insight, what do we have finally?
If I ignore him he won't prepare my taxes—
How no one warned us analogies weren't true,
He rambles on. The damn terriers always win,
I say. Why are you so fitful, so susceptible?
And so on. Pushing my faults around
Like an apple. Rumps of snow,
The furnace pounding, the neighbor's barking
Terrier. She's the one with tattoos
Of bluegills, he says, places you don't
Want to see. Ok, I agree. I'll agree
To anything that doesn't have to do with money.
Nature is rude, decided the Rationalists,
But I was tired of confrontation. Waking
In the middle of the night, the sky calm
With stars, I drank two lemonades I was so thirsty
Listening to Fats Waller on the radio

Late August

Like two 5 dollar whores, he declared,
Stuck in the woods in a truck out of gas.
A halo of talk, a halo of smoke.
How about two women loggers, I suggested.
There aren't many of those, he said,
Besides, they don't run out of gas.
Decay in the corner beyond the pool table.
I didn't expect him to follow me to my car
In the sun and humidity. She complained
Her backside was too flat; last time I saw her
It wasn't. Who are you talking about, I asked.
Your ex-wife, he said. It was disappointing
To see someone like him, his youth blown into patches
Of white sand surrounded by thistle. Adios, I replied.
Back at the cabin monarchs twittered among milkweed.
Along the path to the spring, into a cape of second growth,
A group portrait this side of the great stumps,
Me in a flannel shirt grasping a red container of gasoline.
Purple hollyhocks and pink ones,
Purple to the point of blackness

Part 4

Sand

Water muscling to shore at twilight,
Muscling over her ribs, the water so warm
For September. Thomas Paine said,
We just couldn't stay boys
(regarding the colonists)
Or something to that effect.
Ladybugs gather, covering a peach,
Gulls screech about the deserted lighthouse.
How agreeable to discover
Someone loves you, or even later,
That you've become a fixture
In someone's stable of influences.
As you adjust your sunglasses and sip
Your merlot—a robust season
Of potatoes and cod, when generosity
Was more than a glimmer of an inn's lights.
All this time without a plan or reliable income.
She drives like Barney Oldfield
Says her Dad, arm on my shoulder,
Approaching dust on the beach track.
Just when I thought I was strongest
And most personable

After the Phone Call

She looked nearly the same
But when I hugged her
There was substantially more
To her—no doubt as with me.
She fibbed as I did at the edge
Of curb under the streetlight
As spiders dropped like tiny
Parachutes—they were difficult
To see. On the periphery
Of good luck, I thought,
Revisiting her quirky habits
And expressions, what I eventually
Found so bothersome. Except
When I glanced at my watch
I discovered I was trembling
Like a small-time embezzler.
I see, she said, you must have
An appointment. The driveways
And hedges funneling back
Into darkness, into someone else's
Childhood, where speech was
An obstacle. Wild turkeys
Approaching across the lawn.
Oh no, I said, I'm just so pleased
To see you. But that didn't
Make sense either. She cocked
Her head, a woman with grown
Twins and three conniving husbands.
Even my toes felt damp. I remember,
She said, when you'd lay your head
On my lap, I'd stroke your hair—
I didn't recall. Though I thought

That would be a good idea now.
But I'm married, I said. I own
My own business. It would have
Been helpful if I'd planned
Some banter. I'm a high school
Principal, she told me,
I don't put up with horseshit
From anyone. I brushed the arm
Of her jacket—she merely stared.
A door slammed. A grown idiot
Drooled in an attic somewhere down
The lane. I had another image
As well, one that held an odor
Of patchouli oil. As she stepped
Forward without caution, placed a hand
On my neck. Take me, she insisted,
To those rivets of flame following
Wire—because this is it,
You'll never have another
Hour. I immediately felt
Calmer . . .

1966

On the last 100 degree day for twenty years
My brother returned from Colorado

I was soon in disagreement with him,
Sitting on the porch in my wet swimsuit
I told him what had been bothering me.
You know what that means, he said.
But he didn't care, having a girl he knew
Who worked at the bait shop

He was gone all night, while I sat up
With whiskey.
In the morning the sky a burnt marshmallow texture,
I ate my bluegill fillets, he his frog legs

My bad dreams. His sun-shaped face, and a whistling
Teakettle. Porcelain shadow, a breath of anger
Over water

At that age, my brother knew what he was doing,
I didn't.

Molly

Inviting me into her bed every night
Until she met a mechanic
Who could fix her Volvo.
Not that I didn't understand,
But I was bitter.
Empty, a bit sick
In the kidneys—
Under the swaybacked roof,
Shadows in brown,
This warehouse of silence . . .
My chair beside the woodstove,
Snow melting into rivulets
My coat smoking—even a decade later

~

Weightless insects,
Styrofoam, musk of broken pottery.
I like the way you've thought
This out, you say. I do, she says,
Swim everyday . . .

Shadows and pollen flitting past
A raised window. Loose grasses
Beyond a tiered parking area
For residents—
All of whom have disappeared;
Just tromped over the dune
With picnic baskets and fixed smiles . . .

How did you find me, she asks,
Did someone tell you?

The Friday Night Stripper

A modest brick tavern with quoined corners
(one of three buildings where roads crossed)
A district courthouse when stage coaches stopped
—patched cement steps to double oak doors. While I
Was thirsty and tired. Certainly discouraged.
In my mid-20s I was still susceptible to
A beguiling notion that good things were free
(though evidence kept juddering to the opposite ledger . . .)

⁓

I didn't think she looked like a teacher at all
When she arrived late. The owner tilted his head
As if listening for extinct pigeons, then pointed up the stairs
For the smallish woman with platinum hair.
Oh no, he said, when the dust died,
It's the god's truth, she teaches in a town outside Toronto . . .

In the basement the owner revealed barred cells
Lining both walls, where beer, wine and accessories
Were stored. I had an immediate impression of wet mittens
Holding marshmallows. Mortar turning into suet,
Blackened rocks of nervous nostalgia. This is where
The Americans prisoners were kept, he said,
During the War of 1812 . . .

⁓

She was preceded on stage by a three-piece band
Of guitar, bagpipe and violin . . .

Her breasts beat like clappers.
Then gradually it was night, the owner switched on light.

Among the locals was 200 years of accumulated sweat,
A clock, a bulky cabinet with shelves painted off-white
(which appeared to store discarded items of clothing),
A dozen tables, the shadows of heads like pumpkins . . .

~

I sat with her after a performance, gave her a light.
What grade do you teach, I asked. Any grade you want.
In her robe she shrunk even further. Behind us
The mix of conversations had mostly to do with farming.
I work for a circus, I said. I gave her a free ticket.
Her fingers felt like thin fish, like winter smelt.
Her weak chin wouldn't improve with age either,
I thought. But who was I to monitor possible defects . . .

You're not Canadian, are you, she stated,
Rubbing out her cigarette, her eyes lifting. At the moment
I was more like the rusting weathervane in the corner
Behind the stage. Or the dented pewter pitcher
In her room upstairs. I was in Detroit once, she said . . .

In Her 50s

Sally suspects spiders are making marks
On her legs. Stirring her coffee with a butter knife

An eagle beats south towards the dam
At midday. The shapes of chairs, of towels

The way light pours from the deck—
Unless it is later in the day than she understands—

Everyone was friends once, even lovers were friends,
Then idiosyncrasies appeared like age spots

Angry swans and teeth of muskellunge. Closing the door
Other voices disappear like sound does

When the radio's plug is pulled. Picking up the yardstick,
Blue around the eyes. Goldfinches and hickory nuts

Something so ordinary and calm, like two bottles of shiraz
At rest on the counter. Books and an architect's drawings

But where are the dogs?

~

After the housepainters disappeared (a month before)
Leaving their wooden ladders askew

The strange tips of waves, as in Japanese
Prints. Bug bites, curdled milk

Like sitting in city traffic, the bridge
Rocking from heavy trucks—faint tingle of music

From somewhere—when somewhere else
Is where one wants to be. How one grows accustomed

To certain habits even after one's out-grown them.
Just as she notices how shaggy the trees have become—

After the reception, papers to be signed
An occasional glimpse of a beaver

Padding below the bank to elderberry bushes

~

Lying out on the grass as she once did
When everyone was pleased. When nothing was ever

Put away. Did you sleep with him, her sister asked.
What do you think? she replied

Holding the hairbrush, waving the hairbrush
Her sister shrunk to the size of an antelope—

Plans liquefied, trickled into sand,
Left clumps

Like water which had held paint brushes in a coffee can

Waiting for Someone

On the bulkhead over the bar
Names of steamers that used to stop here

The river silted with new islands and old tires

I've been postponing this drink for hours
She says, though I hadn't inquired

~

Across the alley where the train station
Once held court, exposed brick, hardwood floors

Where I stood at the entrance, five years old,
My hand in my mother's, redcaps pushing carts

Steam rising, throbbing train engines
Aiming north or south, hissing and blowing

Flurry of snow, so much authority among
The businessmen, women in mink, conductors

~

Don't pay attention to Harold, she insists
He isn't tactful, he isn't anything

But I was studying the smoke stained
Painting beyond the bottles and mirrors

A woman examining her shoulder for freckles
Or bruises, in a perilous boredom

Once, years earlier, I had contemplated
Stealing it

~

Even monotony has moles, places where hair grows.

I thought she might hit him with her glass

But Harold vanishes for cigarettes

~

An iron tint to the water, just before freezing rain
Crosses the city pond with a crisp leaf or two

~

Feigning indifference, knowing where irony lay

Next thing you're babbling like an escaped convict
After a six-pack has gone down his gullet

~

Cabbages in snow, old ladies with dull stories,
Crested birds popping rotten red berries

But you get my drift, I can't recall if I
Was up north or not, or even married.

Then a tall man pushing through the festooned door
Resembled my father, when I hadn't had such a thought

In weeks

Light

The young women think they're special
I've got news for them said Margie

Shortly thereafter Margie died—
So that acquaintances in time actually

Forgot her name. Even me
Until several years later

Sitting against a briny log on a beach
In Oregon fiddling with a jacket zipper

~

A gaggle of struggling stock brokers
That winter in San Francisco, an inexplicably

Emotional bunch packed in a building
Where I'd rented a room—a solitary redwood

In the courtyard that no one could see
From the street

Waiting for something to happen

~

I tossed my cowboy boots

Bought new sunglasses. Purchased
A battery for the pickup—in Mendocino

Or maybe Fort Bragg a man with a parrot
On his shoulder winked at me from a bar stool

A 12-year-old girl lounging at the pool table
Ran her small hands up and down a cue stick

Wearing tight white shorts—I just wanted to sit
And stare at the ocean, like anxious civilians

After Pearl Harbor, especially when a Japanese
Pilot bombed the lookout tower on Mt. Emily

Outside of Brookings—which is where I was heading
After Sterry had notified me of a job at his brother's theatre—

Why I was smoking my last cigarette
In the wind and haze, a view to sea-stacks. No back story

No nothing.
But blessed with a fundamental freedom. At least until dinner

　　　⌇

Margie on her bicycle
With sodden groceries in her basket—her mind full of

Adventure at that point. Blouse and skirt clinging

At an intersection up from the lake.
When the sun flashed out, a sheen

On water, a blitz of chrome, image of a boat,
Like a scene in a French movie popular at the moment

On art house screens. How some passions decline, while others perk up

Like various game fish along the weed line of a Midwestern
Stretch of water. No, she wasn't the romantic type

But there was a sensation
Something massaging the surface of things, the future for instance

Even if fence lines were out of kilter, down by the bend
By the beeches

Where the road petered out

Acknowledgments

Grateful acknowledgment is given to the publications
in which the following poems first appeared.

After Lunch—*Fail Better*
After the Phone Call—*Poetry*
The Beast—*History of Lincoln Lake*
Bones in the Trout Pond—*The Bulletin, Giants Play Well In the Drizzle,*
    Peaches
Bug Bites—*Saint Ann's Review*
A City—*Laurel Review*
Commerce—*Grand Street*
The Confession—*Fail Better*
Cottage in the Country—*London Review of Books*
Craters—*Bald Ego*
Dan and Marcia—*Poetry*
Dated—*Jejune*
A Day at the Races—*Poetry*
Fishing at the Falls—*London Review of Books*
The Fondness—*London Review of Books*
The Friday Night Stripper—*Poetry*
Getting Purchase on Ice—*Grand Street*
The Interview—*Bald Ego*
Joke—*Fail Better*
Late August—*Laurel Review*
Local History—*Poetry*
Molly—*Driftwood*
Muscle—*Poetry*
1966—*Exquisite Corpse*
Of the River—*Bald Ego*
Oregon—*Epoch*

Outside Indianapolis—*Saint Ann's Review*
Substation—*Salt Lick, Peaches*
Painting Shutters—*Grand Street, New Poems From The Third Coast*
Restorations—*London Review of Books*
Sand—*London Review of Books*
Sardines and Pears—*Mudfish*
A Snowy Evening—*Poetry*
Time—*Shade*
Toucans—*London Review of Books*
A Town—*London Review of Books*
Turning 50—*Shade*
Under the Sky—*London Review of Books*
The Visit—*Saint Ann's Review*
Waiting for Someone—*London Review of Books*
Water—*Driftwood*
Whispering—*London Review of Books*
Willow—*Epoch*

About the Author

Robert VanderMolen has been publishing poetry in periodicals since the mid-1960s.

His first collection, *Blood Ink*, appeared in 1967. After receiving degrees from Michigan State University and the University of Oregon and employment in a number of interesting occupations, he taught at Grand Rapids Community College for a few years until deciding to open his own business as a painting contractor. He was awarded an NEA Fellowship in 1995. His poetry has appeared in such periodicals as *Poetry, Epoch, Jacket, Parnassus, Grand Street, Sulfur, London Review of Books*, and *The Michigan Quarterly Review*. Previous collections include *Breath, Along the River, Circumstances, The Pavilion*, and *The Lost Book*; chapbooks include *Of Pines* and *Night Weather*. VanderMolen lives in Grand Rapids, Michigan.